YOUR KNOWLEDGE HAS VALUE

Mathias Riechert, Xiaomin Su, Han Chen Hsu

Influence Factors For Online Dating Profit

GRIN Publishing

Bibliographic information published by the German National Library:

The German National Library lists this publication in the National Bibliography; detailed bibliographic data are available on the Internet at http://dnb.dnb.de .

Imprint:

Copyright © 2010 GRIN Verlag, Open Publishing GmbH
Print and binding: Books on Demand GmbH, Norderstedt Germany
ISBN: 978-3-640-91244-5

This book at GRIN:

http://www.grin.com/en/e-book/171760/influence-factors-for-online-dating-profit

GRIN - Your knowledge has value

Since its foundation in 1998, GRIN has specialized in publishing academic texts by students, college teachers and other academics as e-book and printed book. The website www.grin.com is an ideal platform for presenting term papers, final papers, scientific essays, dissertations and specialist books.

Visit us on the internet:

http://www.grin.com/

http://www.facebook.com/grincom

http://www.twitter.com/grin_com

INN342
Enterprise Data Mining and Data Analysis

Case Study 4

Online Dating Website Data Mining Project

STUDENT NAMES: XIAOMIN SU
                 HAN CHEN HSU
                 MATHIAS THOMAS RIECHERT

TABLE OF CONTENTS

TABLE OF FIGURES

1 INTRODUCTION

'. . . Knowledge Discovery is the most desirable end-product of computing. Finding new phenomena or enhancing our knowledge about them has a greater long-range value than optimizing production processes or inventories, and is second only to task that preserve our world and our environment. It is not surprising that it is also one of the most difficult computing challenges to do well . . .' (Wiederhold, 1996).

The main objective of knowledge discovery in Data Mining lies in the finding of data patterns. The knowledge about the current customers can be used to predict profitable customers based on their personal information. This explorative report focuses on analysing different methods of data mining to predict profitable customers of a dating site. The second key aspect is to match individual customers based on their personal information.

The dataset analysed is derived from the customer database of Australia's largest dating site with over 1.9 million members. The dataset contains static activity and dynamic activity. Static activity includes all personal, demographic and interest information entered by the customer at its registration. The emails sent, channels communicated and kisses sent describe the dynamic activity.

Static Activity	Dynamic Activity
Sexuality	Been Viewed
Eye colour	Profile Viewed
Hair colour	Channels Initiated
Star sign	Channels Received
Ethnic Background	Emails Sent
Have Children	Emails received
Personality	Kisses sent
Smoke	Kisses received
Religion	
Want Children	
Education	
Politics	
Diet	
Height	
Drink	
Age Group	
Industry	
Occ Level	
Marital Status	
Body type	
Sexuality	

Table 1: Customer details

Table 1 shows the customer details in the table. Another data table holds the information for users without stamps.
The given data offers various topics to be analysed:

- How do users interact?
- Who is likely to pay money based on static behaviour?
- Who is likely to pay money based on dynamic behaviour?
- What makes a person purchase a stamp?

Based on these questions, the resulting report outline for this document is:

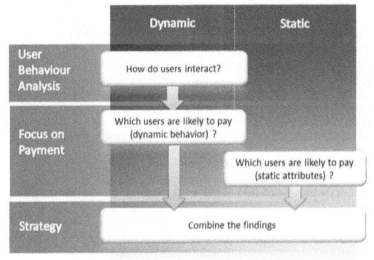

Figure 1: Report outline

The basis for the report is the user behaviour analysis. After a general analysis the focus is laid on determining which users are likely to pay for the service. This includes dynamic and static data. In the final step the combination of the findings is used to propose an implementation strategy for the future development of the website.

2 RELATED WORK

Online social networks and identity representation are active research areas with input from computer sciences, statistics, sociology and psychology. Studies on psychological aspects of social identity representation examine the social implication of displaying public identities (Donath, 2004). The aim of this paper is the analysis of the interactivity between the users of an online dating website and how that influences their payment behaviour.

Toma (2008) addresses the self-presentation issue by observing the characteristics of users to establish the truth about online dating profiles. Hu and Zeng (2007), also use a framework to predict users' identity upon their self-presentation history. While their proposed algorithm achieved high accuracy on prediction, their method is not able to clarify if the predicted traits are real or fabricated.

There are some recent academic studies on online social interaction using popular networks. Carverlee and Webb (2008) studied the characteristic of MySpace profiles based on facets of this social network. This paper has similarity to our work, however the focused was to identify elements of sociability and explain the use of language within different type of gender. The works on other social networks such as Facebook also focus on identity presentation and information sharing in student networks. Acqusiti & Gross (2006) and Tufekci (2008) also examined the disclosure behaviour on MySpace and Facebook users in correlation to privacy issues. The authors proposed a methodology for clustering and identifying similarity in user's behaviours on YouTube data. Lerman and Jones (2006) used a small data sample from Flickr and found that the social network is used to locate new content in the site. Nowwell (2003) investigated co-authorship networks in physics to test how well different graph proximity metrics can predict future collaborations.

The paper at hand focuses on analysing the monetary aspect of an online dating website based on the user profiles. The company will benefit from the resulting prediction rules. Similar to the work of Carverlee and Webb the basis is the analysis of the user behaviour. This is extended by a more prediction-orientated analysis, not to be found before in scientistic literature in the context of dating websites. Accordingly, the website can develop a focus on the target customers and try to attract the potential customers.

3 CONCEPTUALIZATION OF PROCESSES OF DISCOVERY

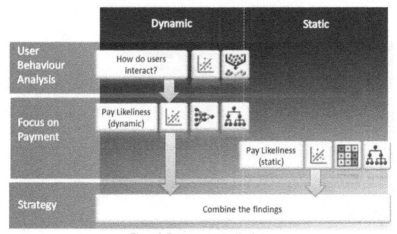

Figure 2: Process conceptualization

Figure 2 depicts the process conceptualization of the report. Its structure is based on Figure 1. For the User Behaviour Analysis the first overview is done with a Regression Analysis. It is used to show the influence of the different behaviour attributes. Regression is a powerful tool to analyse data with interval target variables ("Stamps"). It requires the data to be cleaned before. So missing values have to be imputed and skewed variables have to be modified to achieve a good result. Afterwards a Cluster Analysis helps categorizing and analysing the data more detailed. The resulting behaviour is explained in written form to build the basis for the next steps of the analysis.

In the second step the focus is laid on the payment aspect. The aim is to analyse which customers will pay for the service based on the dynamic and static behaviour. The Neural Network is used to classify the data and give an indication which variables are relevant. The Decision Tree is used to compare the results of classification.

In the third step the resulting rules are combined to form a rule set predicting the likeliness of the customer with special data to use money. In the last step the rule set is converted into an implementation proposal.

Method	Prerequisites	Details	Decision
Regression	• Target variable • Data distribution • Imputation of missing data • Transformation	Regression models outline the relationships among variables to predict or estimate the value of variables. The variables could be age group, kiss received, kiss sent and want children. Analysing the relationship between the stamps and the static data offers the possibility to predict potential profitable customers.	The regression is suited good for prediction. This method is therefore part of our analysis.
Decision Tree	• Target variable • No imputation needed • Data Distribution	Decision Trees are easy to understand and interpret. It consists of nodes and directed edges forming the tree together based on a computed hierarchy. Decision tree works for both categorical and quantitative data and it can grow to any depth, it is also relatively faster than other classification models[1]	Decision Tree models are optimized for classification and prediction. It therefore is part of the analysis.
Neural Networks	• Target and input variables • Data distribution (training and validation) • No transformation needed • No imputation needed	Neural Networks are another approach used for prediction. The variables are bound to intern neurons and calculated adaptive. The output layer presents the weight and the coefficients computed by the model.	As Neural Networks can be used to predict customers in a dataset with many variables it is used as a part of the analysis in this report.

[1] (Nayak, 2010)

Method	Prerequisites	Details	Decision
Cluster	• Target variable • Input variable • Change the measurement	Clustering analysis suits the best as the data needs to cluster into groups without the aid of a target variable. Our task analysis result can segment the data into groups that are similar according to these input attributes including age group, kisses been sent and numbers of channel initiated The result of the analysis will allow the company to evaluate the potential profit of prospects from the list as well as for specific segments. Observe that all variables of "dynamic activity" and "not bought stamps" tables except userID and Age should be set as input.	It's the best method for showing the prospect customers by segmenting the data into groups. Still there is no target focus in this method, so it is not suited to analyse if the customer will buy.
Link Analysis	• ID variable • Target Variable (Nominal or Ordinal) • (Sequence var.)	The Link Analysis discovers links between variables according to a set of records in a data set. [2] It would be possible to link transform the data into an association analysis by creating a new target variable. It contains all characteristics of one variable. Each characteristic gives a new line, so the characteristic count should be reduced by bucketing. It still gets a very large Table and the calculation can take long. The resulting analysis shows which of the attributes are most likely to go together. That is good to get to know your customers, especially when focused on people with a very extensive stamp buying behaviour and their counterparts. So strategic decisions can be made how to address a special user field.	The resulting data brings many rules, showing the nature of the customers in a unstructured way. For this purpose Decision trees are fitted better.

Table 2: Method alternatives

---

[2] (Nayak, 2010)

4 PRE-PROCESSING AND POST-PROCESSING

The first step is to get the Data from the Excel Files into SAS. This is done by using the Extract – Transformation – Load Process.

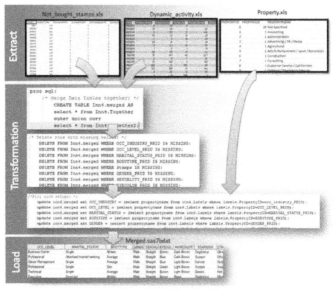

Figure 3: Data Preparation

The active and passive data is merged together from the files "Not_bought_stamps.xls" and "Dynamic_activity.xls" with an outer union. Afterwards the lines with missing values are deleted. This ensures every Data Mining Method to be applicable. Out of 101243 rows 7191 were removed (7%). Imputing data would be possible, but as only 7% of 101243 cases contain missing fields, deleting them still leaves a very high number of cases. The next step resolves the ID's from Property.xls into the database that the information is easier to read. The variable "stamps_YN" holds the binary information if stamps are paid or not. The final table Merged.sas7bdat holds the static information in nominal form and the dynamic information in interval format.

The complete SAS and SQL codes can be found in Appendix - Proc SQL on page 24.

To analyse the dynamic behaviour in Chapter 5, the dynamic variables have to be bucketed to get make the decision tree results more useable.

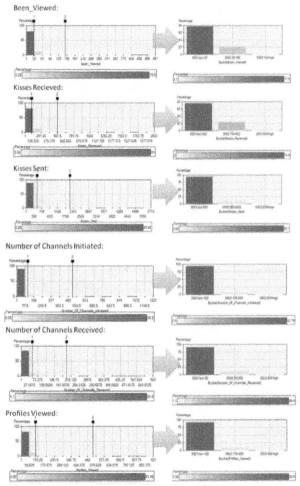

Figure 4: Bucket transformation (behaviour variables) for Decision Tree

5 APPLICATION

5.1 How do users interact?

The starting point of our analysis is the behaviour of the website users. The most important task is to identify user groups to tell how they interact. So the first step is to find out which attributes are good dividing measures to analyse the data.

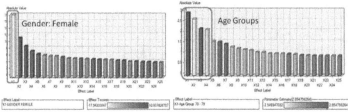

Figure 5: Regression Analysis with the variable „Stamps" as target

Figure 5 shows the results of the Regression Analysis. The target variable is Stamps. It is clearly visible that gender has a high negative influence (highest T-Score value -18%). The analysis of the Estimate values shows a high influence of the age (the first 4 bars are different age groups) variable. These two variables will be the analysed more detailed with the usage of the cluster analysis.

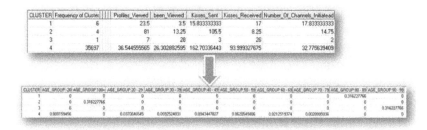

Table 3: Frequency Activity of Cluster

In statistics of table 2, it is clear that the most frequency activity is cluster 4 and from the table 1, we know most of our customers are from the age group 30 to 39 and 40 to 49.

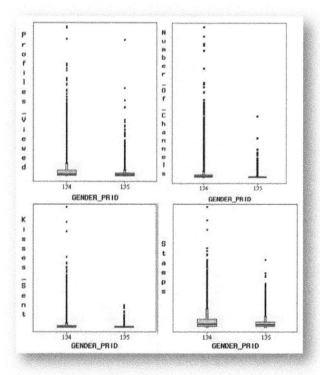

Figure 6: Compare the Activity between Male and Female

Figure 6 compares the activity between Male (134) and Female (135). Males are more active than females; they take the initiative of the dating.

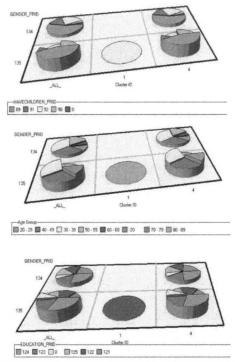

Figure 7: Compare the Kiss Received of Male and Female in different Social Status

- 89:no.
- 90:have children living at home.
- 91:have children living at home sometimes
- 92:have children who don't live at home

- 121:high school

- 122:some college
- 123:diploma
- 124:degree
- 125:post graduate

The reported gender differences did emerge in the social acceptability data, where females indicated more tolerance for social status such as old age and have children. In what may be a surprising finding, females did not report more tolerance for education attractiveness. Conversely, males indicated less tolerance on age and have children status.

Male	Female
is more likely to <u>send</u> kisses and channels	Is more likely to <u>receive</u> kisses and channels
with status of <u>have children, older and high education</u> are more popular.	With status of <u>no children, younger and low education</u> are more popular.

Table 4: Section Result

5.2 Which users are likely to pay based on dynamic data?

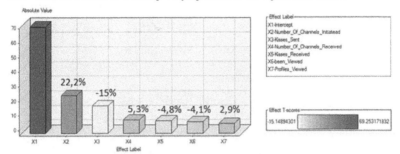

Figure 8: Regression Analysis results

Figure 8 shows the results of the Regression Analysis. Input variables are the dynamic variables in the data set: Number_of_Channels_initiated (X2), Kisses_Sent (X3), Number_of_Channels_Reveived (X4), Kisses Received (X5), been_Viewed (X6) and Profiles_Viewed (X7). The Intercept variable is generated automatically by the Node and does not give new information. The target variable is Stamps in interval.

Short	Variable	T-Score
X1	Number_of_Channels_initiated	22,2 %
X4	Number_of_Channels_Received	5,3 %
X7	Profiles_Viewed	2,9%
X6	been_Viewed	-4,1 %
X5	Kisses Received	-4,8%
X3	Kisses_Sent	-15 %

Table 5: Influence of dynamic variables

Table 5 shows the variables sorted by their influence. X1 cannot be used to predict the stamp usage because the usage of the channels is only possible if stamps were bought. As a result, it is a false predictor and its influence is not revealing new information. Summarising, it can be said that the number of received channels and the number of viewed profiles have a slightly positive correlation with the stamp buying. People, who are often viewed, often kissed and send many kisses are less likely to pay for stamps.

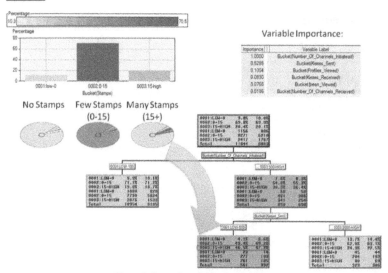

Figure 9: Dynamic variables decision tree

Figure 9 depicts the decision tree for the given data. Before this data can be analysed with a decision tree, the behaviour variables categories have to be separated into buckets (See Figure 4, Page 8). Despite the differences of the bucketing the variable importance order is only slightly changed (See Figure 8, Page 12). The Figure shows that few stamps are the most common way of payment. Furthermore it documents that many stamps are bought by a special behaviour group. Resulting on the given data it has to be decided if the focus is laid on addressing the users who have paid for many stamps or all of who have purchased stamps (Few + Many).

Attribute	Condition
Many Stamps:	
Kisses Sent	0-500
Number of Channels Initiated	100-500 or 500+ → 100+
Few Stamps:	
Number of Channels Initiated	0-100

Table 6: Behaviour variable rules for addressing users buying many stamps

If the aim is to analyse them together, the rules have to be combined with a logical "AND"-operator. The "Number of Channels Initiated" rules condensed give all cases, so this rule can be dropped.

Evaluation of behaviour findings:

Category	General	Many Stamps rules	Many + Few Stamps rules
Cases altogether:	100% (11844)	100% (561) = 4.7% of total	100% (11515) = 97,2% of total
Percentage no stamps:	9.8% (1161)	4.1% (23)	9.6% (1107)
Percentage few stamps (<=15)	69.8% (8267)	49.4% (277)	70% (8065)
Percentage many stamps (>15)	20.4% (2416)	46.5% (261)	20.3% (2343)

Table 7: Rules Evaluation

As the application of the Decision Tree method shows, categorising users based on their flirt behaviour is a non-trivial task. If the rules are applied, a much smaller data set is derived in which "many stamps buying" customers have a much higher stake (46.5%). Because this rule only leaves 261 of 2416 (≈10%) customers in, focusing on that very small group is too specialized. The second possibility is to focus on the many and few stamps buyers as one group. The advantage of this approach is that most of the paying customers are included (97.4%). Furthermore the false-predictor rule "Number of Channels Initiated" is ignored by logical operations. The problem is that only 3% of all cases are excluded, and those excluded are not only customers not paying stamps. Summarizing one can say the given data can't show significant behaviour categories for people to buy stamps. Still, there is a tendency visible connected to the amount of kisses sent. The regression analysis and the Decision Tree have both shown that customers who will send high amounts of kisses are less likely to pay for the service.

As this is the basic finding of the rule resulting for "Many + Few Stamps", this rule will be considered in the combination of rules in the combining chapter.

5.3 Which users are likely to pay based on static data?

The first overview is gained by a Regression Analysis:

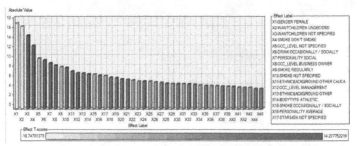

Figure 10: Regression Analysis for static variables

The Figure 10 shows a very high amount of different possible variables. Regression Analysis handles nominal input data this way. As a result it is not optimal for analysing the static aspects of the variables. Still it is clear to see that the variables "Gender", "Want Children", "Smoking Habits" and "Occupancy Level" have a high influence on the stamp buying. The most important assertion is the fact that females are less likely to buy stamps than men. That can be explained by the initiative behaviour of the man (as discussed in 5.1.).

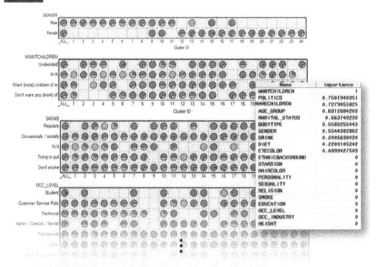

Figure 11: Nearest Neighbour Cluster Results for static variables

Figure 11 shows the results of the Cluster Analysis using SOM. In the given data set 24 clusters are generated. That makes precise analysis unclear. While the first line with the "Gender" variable clearly shows that females are less likely to pay money, the complexity of the attribute characteristics makes a clear statement impossible. Cluster models are good to create a prediction models. Still they lack transparency to understand why cases are classified together. Neural Networks offer even less transparency (Nayak, 2010). As a result the usage of cluster algorithms can be implemented to check for alternative prediction models. As the goal of this paper is to extract prediction rules and to give an insight on the correlated reasons, the usage of a decision tree is more suitable.

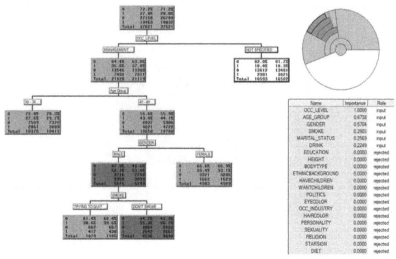

Figure 12: Decision Tree application

Figure 12 depicts the application of the decision tree on the merged data. The target variable is if a customer will pay for the dating service or not. The tree shows that there is a certain group of attributes indicating that this customer will pay. Furthermore it's also visible which group is most likely not to pay any money for the service. The table on the side shows the importance of the attributes based on the decision tree algorithm. The highest influence has the variable OCC_Level (1). All variables listed after Education have no influence.

The classification rules can be extracted from the tree and be used to implement a direct recommendation function for special target groups. The Rules for the group most likely to pay money for the service are shown in the following table:

Attribute	Condition
OCC_Level	Management or Business Owner or Technical Professional
Age_Group	40-49 or 50-59 or 60-69 or 70-79
Gender	Male
Smoke	Don't Smoke or Not Specified

Table 8: Rules for the customer group most likely to pay money

It is interesting that the most important criterion is the variable Occupancy Level. That differs from the results of the Regression and Cluster Analysis. It is explainable by the different ways the algorithms are working. As the tree shows, it is a very good measure to split the data. To get the group with the lowest likeliness only this variable has to be analysed. If it holds one of the values: Not Specified, Customer Service, Admin, Clerical, Secret, other, Student, the person won't pay money with 82% probability. To analyse the structure of the paying better, the next criteria are Age_Group and Gender. It is not surprising that customers above 40 are more likely to pay for a dating service than younger people, because they have more money available, are more likely to be separated and have fewer possibilities to meet other people with shared interests in other ways. The gender decision could be explained by the traditional role of the man to be active in the flirting process. The marital status excludes the married and relationship option. Maybe that can be explained by the lack of seriousness if the person is already married.

Evaluation of static attributes findings:
To evaluate which split is the best, three alternatives are considered:

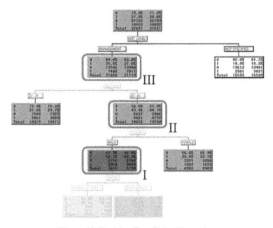

Figure 13: Decision Tree Rule Alternatives

Category	General	I	II	III
Cases altogether:	37621	5675	10658	21028
Percentage no stamps:	72.2% (27158)	47.9% (2718)	56.6% (6032)	64.4% (13542)
Percentage stamps:	27.8% (10463)	52.1% (2957)	43.4% (4626)	35.6% (7486)

Table 9: Static Rules Evaluation

The evaluation shows that the quality of the resulting data is indirectly correlated with the size of the resulting data. If the goal is to find attributes which identify potential buyers with the highest probability solution I is the best, because 52% of the contained cases will buy stamps. Because only 2957 users are left in that classification, only 28% of all stamp buyers are included. The opposite approach (III) is to keep many buyers (75%) but make the sample more heterogenic. That leads to only few resulting rules. By choosing the second alternative (II) nearly the half of the target group is included, and the resulting rules give a better understanding on what it depends if the user buys stamps. This decision has to be assessed in every data mining approach and cannot be generalized. In the given case knowledge discovery is more important than direct marketing scoring, so including only 28% of the relevant target group for the sake of getting more information on which attributes they feature is acceptable. Using this procedure, the results have to be considered as implications rather than 100% - separation rules.

5.4 Combine the findings

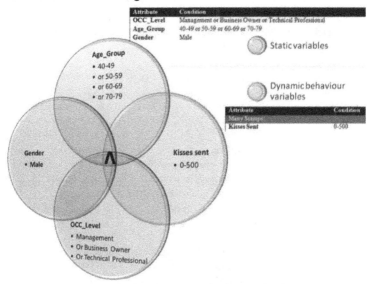

Figure 14: Classification / Prediction Rules combined

The Figure 15 depicts the combination of the rules identified in the steps above. All rules in of the static variables are combined by the "AND" operator, because only cases where all conditions are true identify potential stamp buyers. The resulting rule can be concatenated to a SQL command:

```
proc sql;
create Table Inn4.paying_customers as
    select * from Inn4.merged where
    /*Static Variables:*/
        OCC_Level= "Management" or OCC_Level="Business Owner" or OCC_Level="Technical Professional"
        AND
        Age_Group="40-49" or Age_Group="50-59" or Age_Group="60-69" or Age_Group="70-79"
        AND
        Gender="Male"
    /*Behaviour Variables:*/
        AND
        Kisses_Sent<500;

quit;
```

The resulting table has 18648 rows where 40% (7313 rows) bought stamps. In the data table merged of the dynamic and static data only 25% of 9405 bought stamps. The resulting rules show the attributes indicating the likeliness to buy stamps.

6   COMPARISON TO TRADITIONAL TOOLS

This project is about who is likely to be the buyer of the online dating website. We made some comparison between SAS and the traditional tool SQL before starting the project. Here are the differences and advantages of Data Mining:

- SAS is very efficient and easy to get summary statistics and do lots of different kinds of analyses.
- Data Mining algorithms are capable of working with huge amounts of data. Our Merged table has 100000+ Cases. Microsoft Excel can only work with 65000 cases.
- The methods used (Regression, Decision Tree, Neural Network, Clustering, SOM) all offer individual benefits. They all have in common that they automate the human way of finding knowledge on a high scale of data amount. Doing this with traditional analysing tools would take much more time.
- Data Mining algorithms explore the data by searching for unanticipated trends and patterns in order to gain understanding and ideas, however, traditional SQL focuses on describing the current status. So data mining techniques enhance the knowledge about the present data by the ability to predict future data. An example is the ruleset obtained by analysing the data.
- Using SAS in particular makes the usage and analysis of data very user friendly. The drag and drop functionality is easy to learn without losing functionality. There is no need to get into detailed algorithm programming to use the structures provided by the software. By the usage of Code this detailed modification is still possible and easy to work with.
- SAS provides more ways to solve missing values which makes the data more accuracy. For example missing data could be imputed based on tree algorithms, ensuring the imputed values be as close to the actual value as possible.

Summarising, it can be said that Data Mining uses computing capacity of modern Information Systems to apply the human process of knowledge finding on a huge amount of data. Some like Neural Networks are even simulating the human brain functionality. The results still have to be examined and evaluated, because the algorithms lack the ability of creative thinking and judgement in their present state of development. On the other hand they offer a much higher speed and data processing volume. Using the human expertise together with Data Mining algorithms offers the possibility to compensate both disadvantages resulting in a higher knowledge gain.

7 CONCLUSION

The report at hand shows the process of identifying patterns in the structure of user data. Analysing the data brought an insight about the behaviour of the website users. The findings clearly document that gender as an influence on behaviour, appeal priorities and stamp buying. Based on this insight the focus was laid on finding out what separates people buying many stamps from people buying not buying stamps.

The Regression Analysis proved to be a good tool to determine which variables have a positive or negative influence on the number of stamps bought. Due to the complexity of the variable structure in the given case the resulting information is not suited good for categorising the data in order to understand the attribute linkage better. To solve that issue the usage of Clusters, Neural Networks and Decision Trees was undertaken. Clusters and Neural Networks proved to be good in building predicting models. All the same, they lack transparency to understand the coherences between the attributes and the resulting behaviour. Decision Trees proved to give the best insight.

Analysing the given dataset showed that the users are very heterogeneous and no clear classification border is possible. Although many implications can be made upon the results, all models misclassification rates vary in the field of 23-40%. The filtered dataset does not include all cases of the users buying stamps. This is caused by the high amount of variables and characteristics included. Using these Data Mining techniques it is possible to gain an insight on the complex and unclear data. It has to be emphasised that the focus on this work is the knowledge gain and rule generation. Cluster and Neural Network methods may get better results in prediction results. The lack of transparency makes it impossible to transfer the findings as easily to other areas as it is possible with Decision Trees.

The resulting rules can be used to categorize users. Additionally it is possible to build SQL commands directly from the rules and apply them to website usage. For example it would be possible to make a special offer directly to people not buying stamps directly after the registration of the person. Another practical usage of the results could be to focus more on the paying customers, or implement customized views on the page for different variables. A good example is age group. As older people are more willing to pay for the service there could be a special view on the page for older persons, using the same architecture, data and application logic. That would increase the acceptance in that field and lead to more users with this attribute. Additionally the results can be used to focus on potential customers better.

The next steps include the implementation of the rules on the website. It is possible to build a program or script that automatically transforms the rule output to SQL commands so that they can be selected and used for website application directly. If the webserver is of decent computing power the direct implementation of further methods can be considered.

REFERENCES

Acquisti, A., Gross, R. (2006). *Imagined communities: awareness, information sharing and privacy on the Facebook.* Retrieved Oct 26, from http://petworkshop.org/2006/preproc/preproc_03.pdf

Caverlee, J., Webb, S. (2008). *A large-scale study of MySpace: Observations and implications for online social networks.* Retrieved Oct 26, from http://faculty.cs.tamu.edu/caverlee/pubs/caverlee08alarge.pdf

D. Liben-Nowell and J. Kleinberg.(2004). *The Link Prediction Problem for Social Networks.* Retrieved Oct 26, from http://www.cs.cornell.edu/home/kleinber/link-pred.pdf

Donath, J., Boyd, D. (2004). *Public displays of connection.* Retrieved Oct 26, from http://smg.media.mit.edu/papers/Donath/PublicDisplays.pdf
Hu, J., Zeng, H. (2007). *Demographic prediction based on user's browsing behavior.* Retrieved Oct 26, from http://www2007.org/papers/paper686.pdf

K. Lerman and L. A. Jones.(2006). *Social Browsing on Flickr. In Proceedings of the International Conference on Weblogs and Social Media.* Retrieved Oct 26, from http://www.mpi-sws.org/~gummadi/papers/Growth-WOSN.pdf

Maia, M., Almeida, V., Almeida, J. (2008). *Identifying user behavior in online social networks.* Retrieved Oct 26, from http://delivery.acm.org/10.1145/1440000/1435498/p1-maia.pdf?key1=1435498&key2=4027618821&coll=GUIDE&dl=GUIDE&CFID=10746 7831&CFTOKEN=79923225

Nayak,R. (2010). *INN342 Enterprise Data Mining Practical Session Slides.*

Toma, C. L., Hancock, J. T., Ellision, N. B. (2008). *Separating fact from fiction: An examination of deceptive self-presentation in online dating profiles.* Retrieved Oct 26, from http://www.cl.cam.ac.uk/~rja14/shb09/hancock2.pdf

Tufekci, Z. (2008). *Can you see me now? Audience and disclosure regulations in online social network sites.* Retrieved Oct 26, form http://userpages.umbc.edu/~zeynep/papers/ZeynepCanYouSeeMeNowBSTS.pdf

Wiederhold,G.(1996). *On the barriers and future of knowledge discovery.* Advances in Knowledge Discovery and Data Mining,ed. Fayyad,UM, Piatetsky-Shapiro,G.,Smyth,P.and Uthurusamy,R.,AAAI Press,Menlo Park,CA.

APPENDIX - PROC SQL

I. Import Data Tables:

Together is the modified dynamic_activity data, together 2 is the modified not_bought_stamps table. Together they form the table merged. (See Figure 3: Data Preparation, Page 7)

```
PROC IMPORT OUT= INN4.dynamic_activity
        DATAFILE= "C:\Documents and Settings\n7638604\Desktop\My Dropbox\INN342\Assignment 4\Data\dynamic activity.xls"
        DBMS=EXCEL REPLACE;
    SHEET="Sheet1$";
    GETNAMES=YES;
    MIXED=NO;
    SCANTEXT=YES;
    USEDATE=YES;
    SCANTIME=YES;
RUN;

PROC IMPORT OUT= INN4.together
        DATAFILE= "C:\Documents and Settings\n7638604\Desktop\My Dropbox\INN342\Assignment 4\Data\ together.xls"
        DBMS=EXCEL REPLACE;
    SHEET="Sheet1$";
    GETNAMES=YES;
    MIXED=NO;
    SCANTEXT=YES;
    USEDATE=YES;
    SCANTIME=YES;
RUN;

PROC IMPORT OUT= INN4.together2
        DATAFILE= "C:\Documents and Settings\n7638604\Desktop\My Dropbox\INN342\Assignment 4\Data\ together2.xls"
        DBMS=EXCEL REPLACE;
    SHEET="Sheet1$";
    GETNAMES=YES;
    MIXED=NO;
    SCANTEXT=YES;
    USEDATE=YES;
    SCANTIME=YES;
RUN;
```

II. Merge together and together2, delete missing rows, include labels:

```
proc sql;
        /* Merge Data Tables together: */
                CREATE TABLE Inn4.merged AS
                select * from Inn4.Together
                outer union corr
                select * from Inn4.Together2;
        /* Delete rows with missing values: */
                DELETE FROM Inn4.merged WHERE OCC_INDUSTRY_PRID IS MISSING;
                DELETE FROM Inn4.merged WHERE OCC_LEVEL_PRID IS MISSING;
                DELETE FROM Inn4.merged WHERE MARITAL_STATUS_PRID IS MISSING;
                DELETE FROM Inn4.merged WHERE BODYTYPE_PRID IS MISSING;
                DELETE FROM Inn4.merged WHERE Stamps IS MISSING;
                DELETE FROM Inn4.merged WHERE GENDER_PRID IS MISSING;
                DELETE FROM Inn4.merged WHERE SEXUALITY_PRID IS MISSING;
                DELETE FROM Inn4.merged WHERE EYECOLOR_PRID IS MISSING;
                DELETE FROM Inn4.merged WHERE HAIRCOLOR_PRID IS MISSING;
                DELETE FROM Inn4.merged WHERE STARSIGN_PRID IS MISSING;
                DELETE FROM Inn4.merged WHERE ETHNICBACKGROUND_PRID IS MISSING;
                DELETE FROM Inn4.merged WHERE HAVECHILDREN_PRID IS MISSING;
                DELETE FROM Inn4.merged WHERE PERSONALITY_PRID IS MISSING;
                DELETE FROM Inn4.merged WHERE SMOKE_PRID IS MISSING;
```

```
          DELETE FROM Inn4.merged WHERE RELIGION_PRID IS MISSING;
          DELETE FROM Inn4.merged WHERE WANTCHILDREN_PRID IS MISSING;
          DELETE FROM Inn4.merged WHERE EDUCATION_PRID IS MISSING;
          DELETE FROM Inn4.merged WHERE POLITICS_PRID IS MISSING;
          DELETE FROM Inn4.merged WHERE DIET_PRID IS MISSING;
          DELETE FROM Inn4.merged WHERE HEIGHT_PRID IS MISSING;
          DELETE FROM Inn4.merged WHERE DRINK_PRID IS MISSING;
          DELETE FROM Inn4.merged WHERE Age_Group IS MISSING;
          CREATE TABLE Work.merged AS
          select * from Inn4.merged;
/*add string columns: */
          ALTER TABLE Work.merged add OCC_INDUSTRY char(25);
          ALTER TABLE Work.merged add OCC_INDUSTRY char(25);
          ALTER TABLE Work.merged add OCC_LEVEL char(25);
          ALTER TABLE Work.merged add MARITAL_STATUS char(25);
          ALTER TABLE Work.merged add BODYTYPE char(25);
          ALTER TABLE Work.merged add GENDER char(25);
          ALTER TABLE Work.merged add SEXUALITY char(25);
          ALTER TABLE Work.merged add EYECOLOR char(25);
          ALTER TABLE Work.merged add HAIRCOLOR char(25);
          ALTER TABLE Work.merged add STARSIGN char(25);
          ALTER TABLE Work.merged add ETHNICBACKGROUND char(25);
          ALTER TABLE Work.merged add HAVECHILDREN char(25);
          ALTER TABLE Work.merged add PERSONALITY char(25);
          ALTER TABLE Work.merged add SMOKE char(25);
          ALTER TABLE Work.merged add RELIGION char(25);
          ALTER TABLE Work.merged add WANTCHILDREN char(25);
          ALTER TABLE Work.merged add EDUCATION char(25);
          ALTER TABLE Work.merged add POLITICS char(25);
          ALTER TABLE Work.merged add DIET char(25);
          ALTER TABLE Work.merged add HEIGHT char(25);
          ALTER TABLE Work.merged add DRINK char(25);
/*fill with values: */
          update Work.merged set OCC_INDUSTRY = (select propertyname from inn4.Labels where
          labels.PropertyID=occ_industry_PRID);
          update Work.merged set OCC_LEVEL = (select propertyname from inn4.Labels where
          labels.PropertyID=OCC_LEVEL_PRID);
          update Work.merged set MARITAL_STATUS = (select propertyname from inn4.Labels where
          labels.PropertyID=MARITAL_STATUS_PRID);
          update Work.merged set BODYTYPE = (select propertyname from inn4.Labels where
          labels.PropertyID=BODYTYPE_PRID);
          update Work.merged set GENDER = (select propertyname from inn4.Labels where
          labels.PropertyID=GENDER_PRID);
          update Work.merged set SEXUALITY = (select propertyname from inn4.Labels where
          labels.PropertyID=SEXUALITY_PRID);
          update Work.merged set EYECOLOR = (select propertyname from inn4.Labels where
          labels.PropertyID=EYECOLOR_PRID);
          update Work.merged set HAIRCOLOR = (select propertyname from inn4.Labels where
          labels.PropertyID=HAIRCOLOR_PRID);
          update Work.merged set STARSIGN = (select propertyname from inn4.Labels where
          labels.PropertyID=STARSIGN_PRID);
          update Work.merged set ETHNICBACKGROUND = (select propertyname from inn4.Labels where
          labels.PropertyID=ETHNICBACKGROUND_PRID);
          update Work.merged set HAVECHILDREN = (select propertyname from inn4.Labels where
          labels.PropertyID=HAVECHILDREN_PRID);
          update Work.merged set PERSONALITY = (select propertyname from inn4.Labels where
          labels.PropertyID=PERSONALITY_PRID);
          update Work.merged set SMOKE = (select propertyname from inn4.Labels where
          labels.PropertyID=SMOKE_PRID);
          update Work.merged set RELIGION = (select propertyname from inn4.Labels where
          labels.PropertyID=RELIGION_PRID);
          update Work.merged set WANTCHILDREN = (select propertyname from inn4.Labels where
          labels.PropertyID=WANTCHILDREN_PRID);
          update Work.merged set EDUCATION = (select propertyname from inn4.Labels where
          labels.PropertyID=EDUCATION_PRID);
          update Work.merged set POLITICS = (select propertyname from inn4.Labels where
          labels.PropertyID=POLITICS_PRID);
          update Work.merged set DIET = (select propertyname from inn4.Labels where
          labels.PropertyID=DIET_PRID);
```

```
update Work.merged set HEIGHT = (select propertyname from inn4.Labels where
labels.PropertyID=HEIGHT_PRID);
update Work.merged set DRINK = (select propertyname from inn4.Labels where
labels.PropertyID=DRINK_PRID);
/*delete old unneeded PRID columns: */
alter Table Work.merged drop OCC_INDUSTRY_PRID;
alter Table Work.merged drop OCC_LEVEL_PRID;
alter Table Work.merged drop MARITAL_STATUS_PRID;
alter Table Work.merged drop BODYTYPE_PRID;
alter Table Work.merged drop GENDER_PRID;
alter Table Work.merged drop SEXUALITY_PRID;
alter Table Work.merged drop EYECOLOR_PRID;
alter Table Work.merged drop HAIRCOLOR_PRID;
alter Table Work.merged drop STARSIGN_PRID;
alter Table Work.merged drop ETHNICBACKGROUND_PRID;
alter Table Work.merged drop HAVECHILDREN_PRID;
alter Table Work.merged drop PERSONALITY_PRID;
alter Table Work.merged drop SMOKE_PRID;
alter Table Work.merged drop RELIGION_PRID;
alter Table Work.merged drop WANTCHILDREN_PRID;
alter Table Work.merged drop EDUCATION_PRID;
alter Table Work.merged drop POLITICS_PRID;
alter Table Work.merged drop DIET_PRID;
alter Table Work.merged drop HEIGHT_PRID;
alter Table Work.merged drop DRINK_PRID;
/* add stamps yes no:*/
ALTER TABLE Work.merged add stamps_YN numeric(1);
update Work.merged set stamps_YN=0 where stamps=0;
update Work.merged set stamps_YN=1 where stamps>0;
CREATE TABLE Inn4.merged AS
select * from Work.merged;
quit;
```

IV. Resulting SQL:

```
proc sql;
create Table Inn4.paying_customers as
select * from Inn4.merged where
/*Static Variables:*/
OCC_Level= "Management" or OCC_Level="Business Owner" or OCC_Level="Technical
Professional"
AND
Age_Group="40-49" or Age_Group="50-59" or Age_Group="60-69" or Age_Group="70-79"
AND
Gender="Male"
/*Behaviour Variables:*/
AND
Kisses_Sent<500;

quit;
```